Bigger

This  is **big**. This  is **bigger**.

Look at the pictures in each row.
Circle the picture that is **bigger** than the first picture.

Smaller

This  is **small**. This is **smaller**.

Look at the pictures in each row.
Circle the picture that is **smaller** than the first picture.

Same Size

These  are the **same size**.

Look at the pictures in each box.
Circle the pictures that are the **same size**.

What Is a Square?

A **square** is a **shape** that looks like this.

How many ⬜s can you find? _____

What Is a Rectangle?

A **rectangle** is a **shape** that looks like this. ☐

How many ☐s can you find? _____

5

What Is a Circle?

A **circle** is a **shape** that looks like this.

How many ◯s can you find? _____

What Is a Triangle?

A **triangle** is a **shape** that looks like this.

How many △s can you find? _____

Different

These ⭐⭐ are the **same**. This ⭐ is **different**.

Look at the pictures in each row.
Circle the picture that is **different**.

8

Different

Look at the pictures in each row. Circle the picture that is **different**.

What Belongs?

 A and belong together.

Look at the pictures in each row.
Circle the picture that **belongs** with the first picture.

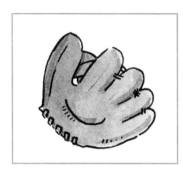
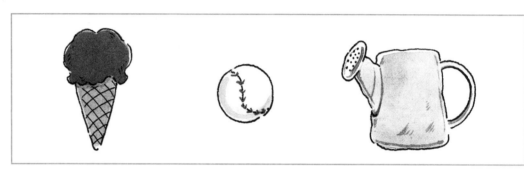

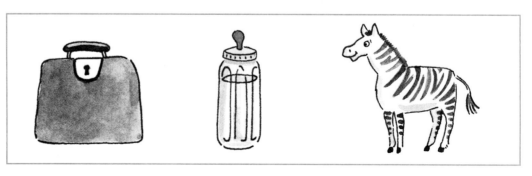

10

What Belongs?

Draw a line from the  below to the pictures that **belong** with it.

What Belongs?

A **belongs** in a .

Draw a line from the  below to what **belongs** in it.

12

What Belongs?

Where does each animal **belong**?
Draw a line from each animal to its house.

Make a Pair

A and a make a **pair**.

A and a do not make a **pair**.

Look at the pictures in each row.
Circle the two pictures that make a **pair**.

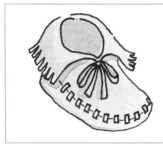   

Make a Pair

A and a make a **pair**.

A and a do not make a **pair**.

Look at the pictures in each row.
Circle the two pictures that make a **pair**.

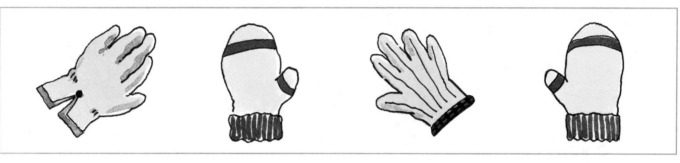

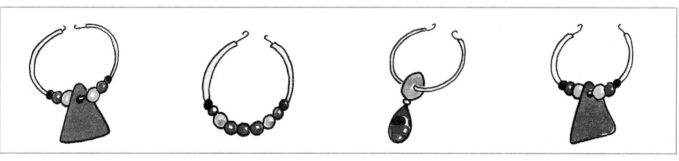

What Is Missing?

Look at the picture.
Then look for the **missing** parts.
Draw in each where it belongs.

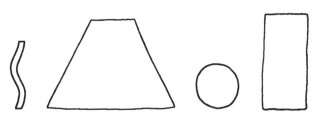

16

What Is Missing?

Look at the picture.
Then look for the **missing** parts.
Draw in each where it belongs.

Opposites

This  is happy. This is sad.

Happy is the **opposite** of sad.

Draw a line from each word to the picture of its **opposite**.

little

night

up

Opposites

Circle the picture that shows the **opposite** of the first picture.

big

soft

 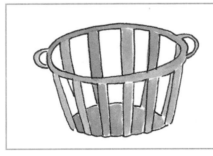 

full

hot

Rhyming

  **rhymes** with .

Say the name of each picture.
Circle the two that **rhyme** in each group.

Rhyming

This  is a hen.

Draw a line from the below to the picture names that **rhyme**.

Which Is Less Than?

Less means **not as many**. 7 is **less than** 8.

Look at the pictures in each row. Circle the set that is **less**.

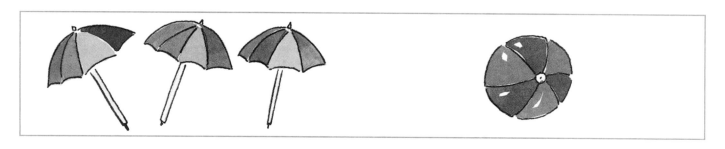

Make a set of s to show 1 **less than** 10.

How many ♥s? _____

Which Is Greater Than?

Greater means **more than**. 8 is **greater than** 7.

Look at the pictures in each row. Circle the set that is **greater**.

Make a set of s to show I **more than** 3.

How many s? _____

First, Next, Last

Write **1** in the square to show what happened **first**.
Write **2** to show what happened **next**.
Write **3** to show what happened **last**.

First, Next, Last

Write **1** in the square to show what happened **first**.
Write **2** to show what happened **next**.
Write **3** to show what happened **last**.

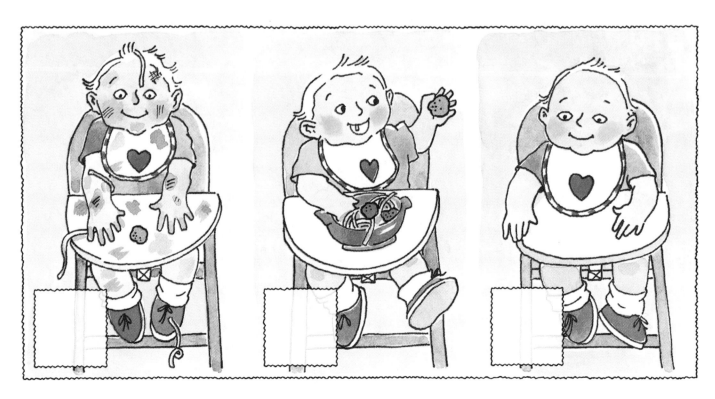

First, Next, Last

Write **1** in the square to show what happened **first**.
Write **2** to show what happened **next**.
Write **3** to show what happened **last**.

26

Before

A comes **before** B.

Write the letter that comes **before** each letter below.

A B C D E F G H I J K L M N O P Q R S T U V W X Y Z

Between

B comes **between** A and C.

Write each letter that comes **between** the letters below.

A B C D E F G H I J K L M N O P Q R S T U V W X Y Z

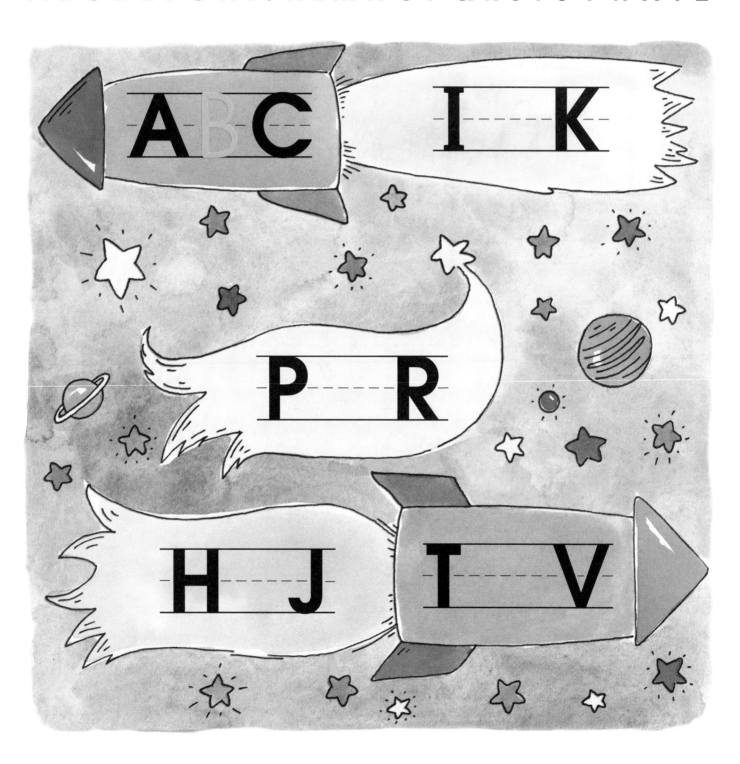

After

C comes **after** B.

Write the letter that comes **after** each letter below.

A B C D E F G H I J K L M N O P Q R S T U V W X Y Z

Letter Match

Look at the ball players. Draw a line from each **uppercase** letter to the matching **lowercase** letter.

A B C D E F G H I J K L M N O P Q R S T U V W X Y Z

a b c d e f g h i j k l m n o p q r s t u v w x y z

Letter Match

Write the matching **lowercase** letter next to each **uppercase** letter.

A B C D E F G H I J K L M N O P Q R S T U V W X Y Z

a b c d e f g h i j k l m n o p q r s t u v w x y z

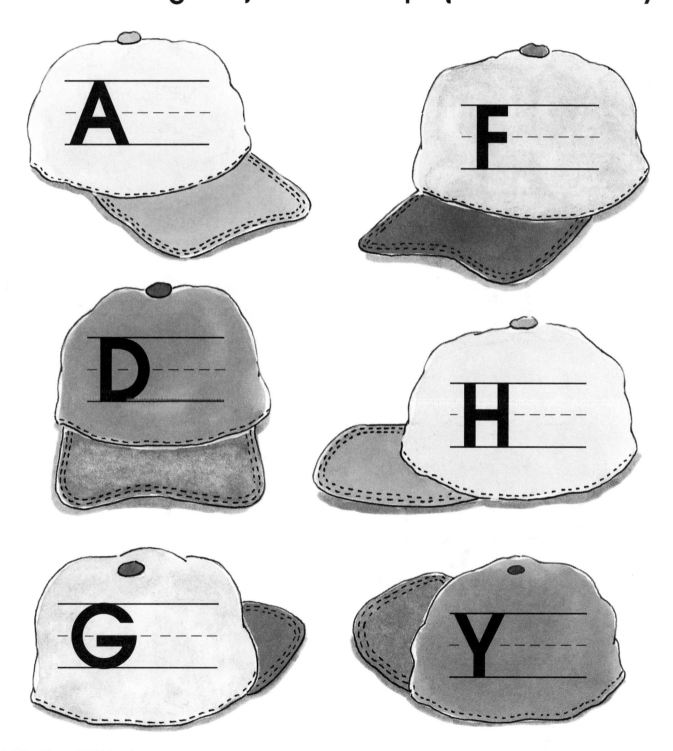

Letter Match

Draw a line from each **uppercase** letter to the **lowercase** letter that matches.

Fill in the Letters

Fill in each blank with the letter that comes **next** in ABC order.

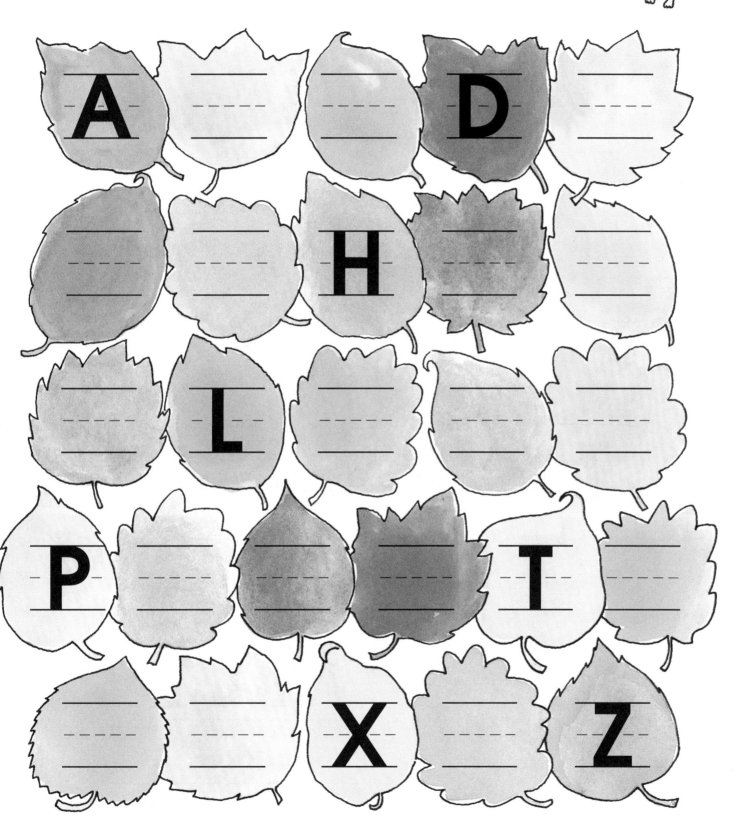

A ___ ___ D ___

___ ___ H ___ ___

___ L ___ ___ ___

P ___ ___ ___ T ___

___ ___ X ___ Z

What Order?

Write each set of letters in **ABC order**.

F E D

P O Q

T S R

M L N

Fill in the Letters

Fill in each blank with the letter that comes **next** in ABC order.

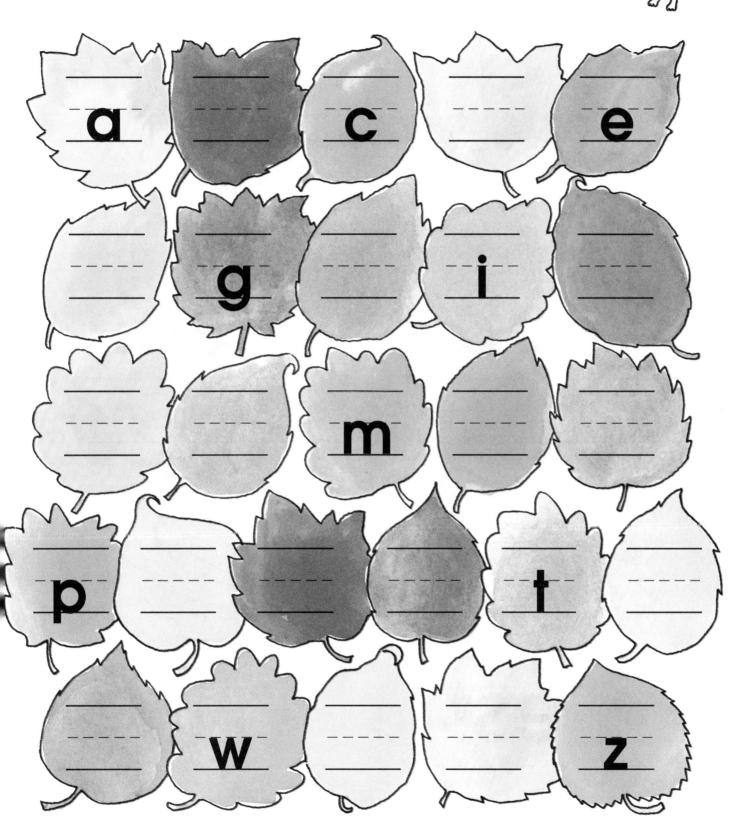

a ____ c ____ e

____ g ____ i ____

____ ____ m ____ ____

p ____ ____ ____ t ____

____ w ____ ____ z

Beginning Sounds

Say the name of each picture.
Write **t** or **n** to begin the word.
Then write the word on the line.

__op

__ent

_____

_____

- - - - - - - - - -

- - - - - - - - - -

_____

_____

__est

__ut

_____

_____

- - - - - - - - - -

- - - - - - - - - -

_____

_____

Beginning Sounds

Say the name of each picture.
Write **m** or **p** to begin the word.
Then write the word on the line.

_m_ **oon**

_____

- - - - - - - - - - -

_____

__ **ig**

_____

- - - - - - - - - - -

_____

__ **an**

_____

- - - - - - - - - - -

_____

__ **an**

_____

- - - - - - - - - - -

_____

Ending Sounds

Say the name of each picture.
Write **d** or **t** to end the word.
Then write the word on the line.

be_d_

_____

- - - - - - - - - - -

_____

goa___

_____

- - - - - - - - - - -

_____

ca___

_____

- - - - - - - - - - -

_____

bir___

_____

- - - - - - - - - - -

_____

Ending Sounds

Say the name of each picture.
Write **m** or **n** to end the word.
Then write the word on the line.

su__

_____

gu__

_____

dru__

_____

fa__

_____

First, Next, Last

Write **1** in the square to show what happened **first**.
Write **2** to show what happened **next**.
Write **3** to show what happened **last**.

40

First, Next, Last

Write **1** in the square to show what happened **first**.
Write **2** to show what happened **next**.
Write **3** to show what happened **last**.

Which Two Go Together?

Draw a line from each **little** picture to the correct **big** picture.

42

Which Two Go Together?

Circle the names of the pictures in each row that **go together**.

hat   bone   dog

shoe   sock   ball

bee   car   flower

bucket   bird   mop

One Does Not Belong

Circle the name of the picture in each row that **does not belong**.

fork	fox	spoon
tree	horn	drum
bed	fan	pillow
box	bat	ball

One Does Not Belong

Circle the name of the picture in each row that **does not belong**.

goat   pig   king

fish   house   barn

apple   bird   orange

hat   coat   cow

Number Words

Color **two** ⭐s yellow.

Color **four** 🪐s blue.

Color **three** 🛸s red.

Color **one** 👽 green.

Number Words

Draw a ◯ around the set of **7**.

Draw a ▢ around the set of **6**.

eight

seven

nine

six

ten

Color the Picture

Color the  **green**.

Color the  **yellow**.

Color the  **blue**.

Color the  **purple**.

Color the  **orange**.

Color the  **brown**.

Color the  **red**.

Color the  **black**.

Leave the  **white**.

48

49

Words That Rhyme

Draw a ◯ around the words that **rhyme** with **sing**.

Draw a ☐ around the words that **rhyme** with **ran**.

fan

ring

man

king

can

pan

swing

50

Words That Rhyme

Draw a ○ around the words that **rhyme** with **sat**.

Draw a ☐ around the words that **rhyme** with **lake**.

snake

cat

cake

mat

rake

bat

hat

Which Is It?

Write the names of the **animals** on the **left**.
Write the names of the **plants** on the **right**.

dog   fish   flower

bush   tree   cow

Animals   Plants

_____   _____

_____   _____

_____   _____

_____   _____

_____   _____

_____   _____

Where Does It Belong?

Draw a line from the **foods** to the .

Draw a line from the **toys** to the  .

apple

berry

doll

jacks

ball

cake

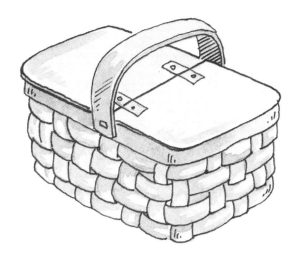

Words

Draw a line from each word to the picture it names.

man

jam

pan

fan

ham

Words

Draw a line from each picture to its name.

hen

goat

men

boat

pen

Where Is It?

over

by

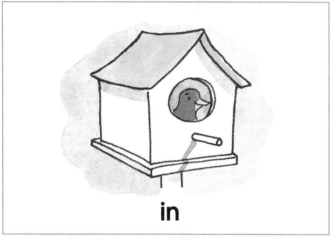

in

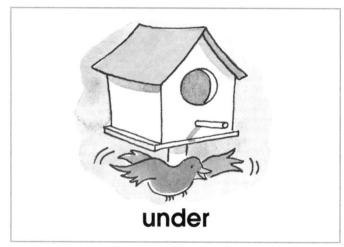

under

Write the word that tells **where** the bird is.

The bird is _____ the .

Where Is It?

The bird is _____ the  .

The bird is _____ the .

The bird is _____ the  .

Where Is It?

on   **by**   **under**

Draw a red 🍎 **under** the 🪑 .

Draw a green 🍏 **on** the 🪑 .

Draw a yellow 🍎 **by** the 🪑 .

58

In, On, and Under

Write the correct **number** on each line.

How many  s are **under** the  ? ______

How many  s are **in** the  ? ______

How many  s are **on** the  ? ______

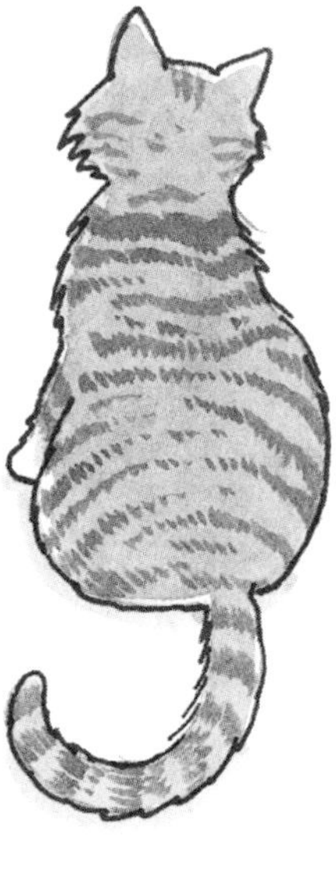

Alphabetical Order

Write the words in **ABC order**.

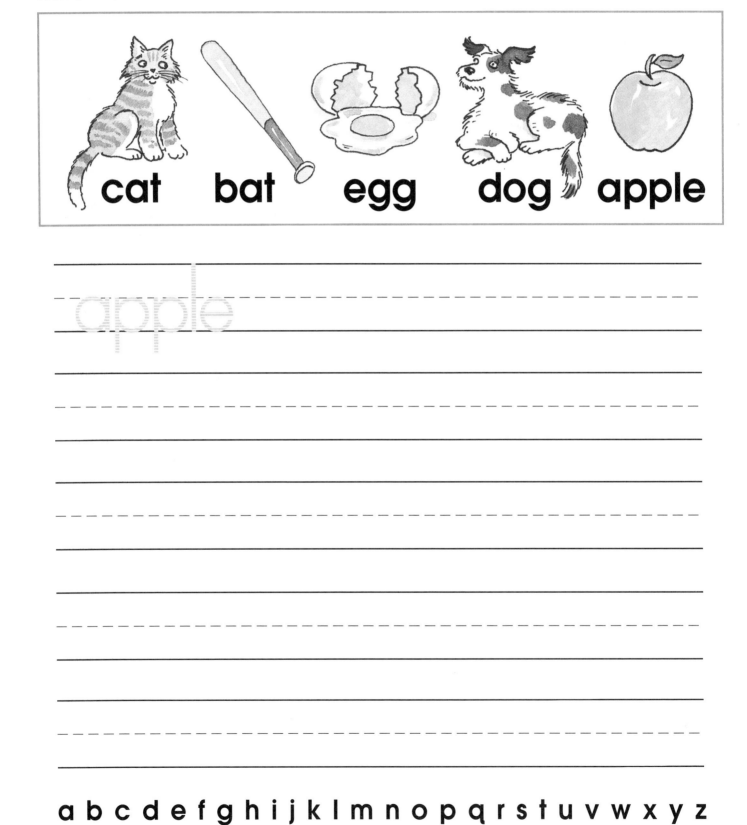

cat   bat   egg   dog   apple

apple

_____

_____

_____

_____

_____

_____

_____

_____

a b c d e f g h i j k l m n o p q r s t u v w x y z

Alphabetical Order

Write the words in **ABC order**.

elf   fox   duck   goat   car

car

a b c d e f g h i j k l m n o p q r s t u v w x y z

What Do You See?

Underline the sentence that **goes with** each picture.

See the ball.

See the dog.

See the doll.

See the ball.

See the boat.

See the dog.

See the doll.

See the boat.

What Do You See?

Underline the sentences that tell what you see.

There are two cows.

There are four balls.

There is a house.

There is one goat.

There is a girl.

Great Job!

YIPEE!

First Name:

Last Name:

has completed **Reading Readiness** from School Zone Publishing.

 Reading Readiness, Grades K–1 02223